Birth of Moses

Om KIDZ
An imprint of Om Books International

After a dreadful draught, the Israelites moved to Egypt and settled there. The Pharaoh was afraid that the Israelites were prospering, multiplying and becoming very strong.

Soon the Pharaoh told his subjects, "We have too many foreigners are dwelling among us. They might turn on us and take control of our land. We must find a way to stop them from becoming too powerful."

The Pharaoh soon declared that all Israelites would be enslaved. The Egyptians made them work hard on construction sites. They were pressed into slavery.

To tackle the increasing population of Israelites, the Pharaoh ordered all the Israelite male babies to be killed. The soldiers ruthlessly snatched the newborn boys and threw them in the Nile.

Jochebed, an Israelite woman, was scared for her baby boy. The mother looked at him and cried, "I do not want to lose my baby, what shall I do?" She hid him for months, but realised that she won't be able to do so for long.

She took a basket made of reed and coated it with pitch to make it waterproof. She placed the baby in it and covered him well. She took the basket to the River Nile and floated it down the river, putting her daughter Miriam, on watch.

The basket flowed in the river and into the Pharaoh's palace. Miriam, who followed her brother from the shore, felt helpless when she saw the basket enter the palace. She hid behind some bushes to see what would happen to her brother.

Pharaoh's daughter, who came there with her maidens to bathe, noticed the basket. One of her maids brought it to her. Seeing the poor little baby crying, she decided to keep him as her son! She called him Moses meaning "drawn out of water!"

Miriam came quickly out of her hiding place and asked the princess, "Would you like me to go and bring an Israelite woman to take care and nurse the baby?" The kind-hearted princess smiled and said, "Yes." Miriam turned and ran home as fast as she could to tell her mother.

When Jochebed came to the palace, the princess told her to take the baby and said, "Keep this baby for me. Take care of him and nurse him. I will pay you well." The mother was so happy that she had tears in her eyes. She took Moses home, so thankful to God that her child was safe.

When Moses grew older, his mother took him back to the princess. The princess accepted him as her son, and Moses started staying with her in the palace.